From the Ashes

Meghan Fogler

Presentation by *BookLeaf Publishing*

Web: www.bookleafpub.com

E-mail: info@bookleafpub.com

ISBN:9789357441742

First edition 2023

DEDICATION

To everyone who is healing

And Mrs. Froehle. I never stopped writing, and you always encouraged me to do so, even 15 years later. Thank you for believing in me.

ACKNOWLEDGEMENT

I'd like to thank my mother, who has always been my rock. I thank my future husband, who has always supported whatever endeavor I chase. My sisters, my cousin Jae, and my cats give me a reason to keep going. None of this would be possible without the publishing company, I am extremely grateful for this opportunity. Lastly, I thank the trees who provide this material for words to be printed and shared. I hope to honor Mother Earth with my words and stories.

PREFACE

Your 20s are shit. I'm not going to lie. No one tells you how rough it actually is...sure there's more adult functioning like paying bills and getting to work on time...but it's the emotional, spiritual, and mental aspects no one talks about.

This is how I processed. These poems are almost 10 years of reprogramming, deconstructing, therapy, and self-discovery. It was an outlet, it was a comfort, it was a necessity.

To anyone in their 20s reading this book...you've got this.

Reality's Witness

Reality is…relative
Reality is…subjective
Reality is…anything but real

I'm pretty sure Toni Jones said that, or something
similar

Whether I'm repeating someone else's words or
philosophy, or rather coming to their realization on
my own accord, I'm not trying to take credit

I'm trying to give it

Give it to all of those creatives and wanderers who
came before

Because what more are we than a conglomerate of
the ones who came before us?

Is anything original? Yes, and no. Non-duality.
Everything and nothing is original. You are unique,
yet time has seen what you have seen through many
cycles…

Reality has always been and will be, but never
witnessed the same as You witness it now

What are you taking time to witness?

Everything I Ever Loved

Everything I used to love
Disappeared into thin air
Once magic, and bliss
Turned to shit

Everything I used to love
It's never as it seems
Once the veil is lifted
You can't even see in between

There's no going back
Even if you try
Begging and pleading, bleeding
Inside and out you cry and cry
But nothing will bring back what's dead inside

There's no resurrection

There's no belief

And when there's no relief, there's no direction

No motivation, no urge, only the desire to purge
and feel anything, including desire

Because what you once loved, you once desired
too. And then you got it, even though it was
taken from you.

The art in museums.
The culture around the block.
Fame and fortune in acting and actresses.
Crystals and crystal shops.
Faith. Yoga. Religion.

The fucking APA.

There's nothing that's not been tainted
By colonialism or the KKK. Capitalism and
patriarchy have ruled for generations, and
continues to spout blasphemy

Everything I ever loved, or believed in to be
true, always had a mask on
Or a veil to be lifted, throwing reality askew
What you once seen can no longer exist, the
blueprint is there but the reality is finished

So what do you do when you're left with
nothing, but the trauma and belief that

Everything you ever loved is a lie

Unspoken Language

Kissing is a language I speak so well

The subtle touch, the smiles, the breathing, the passion
every soft peck, every teeth flick, every lip lick
caressing each other's echoing chambers of vibration and song

Kissing is a language I speak so well

The movements of synchronicity between bodies and tongues
the silkyness of skin underneath cold or rough hands
the gentle and deep eye contact during that moment of pause
when you have to catch your breath

Kissing is a language I used to speak so well

Taking breaths away, ensuing tremors, inducing moans
growing heat and pulsation in regions below
drawing in pressure from body weight and pelvic thrusts

Kissing is an art form that no one practices anymore

Teenage dream, teenage fantasy, teenage desire
knowing no better than to leave behind words and spew truth from the hear
and breath
moments of pure ecstasy, being completely desired and desirable

Kissing is a language I miss so well.

I was fluent in the unspoken.

Scatterbrained

What time is it? 12:54
I need to drop off plastic bags at Meijer
I need to drop off stuff at the vet
I need to find a womens shelter to drop off these
supplies
I need a haircut
I need to go to the laundry-mat and wash all these
damn comforters
I need to clean the bathrooms
I need to clean the kitchen
I need to dust and vacuum and mop
I need to buy garbage bags and peanut oil…probably
can do that at Meijer
We need to get our garden prepped
I need to open the windows and put on the diffusers
I need to sage the house
I need to burn the pile by the fireplace
I need to vacuum the fireplace out
When's the next full moon? My crystals haven't been
charged in a minute...
I have to pay these taxes
I need brakes on my car
I need to buy that plane ticket
I should probably do some grocery shopping but I
have no idea what I want or what we need plus he's
doing his Keto soon so I'm stumped on "meal plans."
We need more shaker bottle lids
What time is it? 12:55

Present Change

Be present in the now.

Focus on Yourself.

Live in the moment.

Change is inevitable.

Either way, there will be an outcome;

Embrace the Experience.

Conversations with YourSelf

You're not invisible. You've got to take care of yourself & be gentle.

How do I do that?

Start by being kind to yourself & love yourself.

How do I do that?

Forgive yourself.

But I don't know how.

Well, how do you forgive someone else?

'Love them anyway'

.

But I don't know how to love myself…

Love. Yourself. Anyway.

Eat Dirt

I am not a Person

I am a Being

Agreeing

Grinning teeth,

Shimmering.

Releasing the rest comes second best
To spinning out of control into a spiral
Knowing no return or force field

Fear not, you have the world in the palm of your
hands
About to enter into your gut as you swallow it
whole

Perspective Pie

If you go through your days with the attitude that you can learn something from every single person you meet, life will become a lot more interesting.

You won't judge as much. You actually WILL learn things you didn't know before.

Every person is a slice of the pie of the perspective of the Universe.

Apply all knowledge and perspective to your experience. Become more aware. Awaken the connection between two spirits finding their way through this physical realm.

Purity Culture

My body was never my own.
       It never belonged to me.

"Don't get pregnant" she said.

It belonged to the "W.E.C" (white evangelical church). It required baptism, a man 65 plus years older than me putting a cloth over my face and submerging me in our baptismal pool in front of dozens of people.

"If you stay under 110 lbs, you can't get pregnant" she said.

It never learned proper boundaries; Daycare experiences shaped that young; Dereks abuse/assault. Middle school ass grabs and slaps out the wazoo.

"Sex before marriage is a sin" they all said.
It learned to survive by manipulating itself to ride those attraction waves, and stay skinny to soar the compliment current.

"If we don't have sex, I won't feel like you're truly mine…you're his" he said.

Her lips were so fucking soft. Her arms around my body, and chest against mine. I was sober. I was 19. But I was straight. I had to be. It's "what I wanted for myself: a husband and kids".

"Everything you've gone through is going to make you such a great mother" too many women have said.

I have been fingered until I bled. I have gotten an STD. I have had an IUD. I have been raped in my sleep, by more than one person. But, I should just sleep with clothes on…that will prevent that from happening, especially subconsciously (i.e. the other person is also sleeping).

"I don't like this" I mumbled with him sitting on my face and his dick down my throat.
"Ugh…but I'm about to finish"as he continued. And I cried, but probably after he was done.

I've had some good experiences. Trust me. O's on O's. No worries. I learned at 9 how to do that for myself.
"Your nipples are showing, put a bra on" he said.

"You're never going out dressed like that" they said, referencing someone else.

"Your dress is see-through as we can see the outline of your legs" they said, while I wore leggings under my dress.
Don't even fucking get me started on sorority recruitment outfit standards and rules. 200 plus dollars a goddamned year. For some bullshit show about how

"We don't judge our girls by how 'pretty' they are", they all said (but at one point did mean).

I've been offered money in exchange for sex. I've only earned $4 on a strip pole though. I thought I was worth more.

"So how many kids do you have?" TOO MANY DAMN PEOPLE HAVE ASKED.

None. I have zero. I now want zero. I don't believe my body would birth a child. And I'm mentally/emotionally unpredictable. Even if I never snapped and left my kids I'd still fuckem'up real good.
"Nude is normal" she says.

"I want you to sit on my face later" he'll say.

"You look healthy" they'll say.

So now even the good things, positive changes still are brought about and done because of other people. My intention is to clearly gain validity in any aspect… Iyengar talks about this exchange concept.
"You need to eat a cheeseburger" they all said.

Meanwhile

"You've got to try this diet and workout you can't just do one or the other" they all keep saying.

Yes, it's always been about balance. I agree with that. But, I ate a Burger King burger every day I worked for almost a

year… it doesn't help you gain weight when it's the
largest/only thing you ate that day.

How do I reclaim my bodily zone? Well.
The universe did that when I graduated.
I've been navigating ever since.

HSP.
Deprogramming.
Reclaiming.
Finding liberation.
Ownership.
Healing.
BEING.

Rock Bottom

Death is the final rest
It's the ultimate release, ultimate relief.
So do not be afraid to live. And it is okay to feel
worn down and recognize when life is kicking
you in the ass.

But when you hit rock bottom, ask yourself if
there's anything more to life you want to
experience. Don't dream about it, and don't give
up. Go. Do. It. It takes work, and work makes
you even more tired, and crave that rest even
deeper. But I promise it's worth it. Sometimes
you don't know how strong you are until you
look back and realize just how far you had to
pull yourself up…

Once you've climbed out of rock-bottom, it's
easier to appreciate yourself and your strength. It
also shows you who has be waiting at the top…
The ones who kept encouraging you to climb. It
also allows you to build emergency brakes on
your way up if you ever started to spiral down
again. The fight is worth it. It gets better… If
you can learn to appreciate yourself and never
give up hope in your recovery.

Find out what works for you, and eventually, the path to rock-bottom will be blown away in the dust you'll be able to see it, remember it, but you literally won't be able to go back. You're too strong at this point. The spirals don't whirl you into the air and toss you down the pit, you hold your ground, and if you can't, can you link a chain to the other people or materials around you to keep you there because you know how, and the work you've put in, has manifested those skills and tools as well as resources necessary to keep you there via those people or things; because they're in the environment you've manifested.

Your body is your world, manifest your reality in this one.

Roots

We are all roots.

Some of us bud, then die. Others bud and flower, and some don't produce at all. The ones that do will produce and thrive, and some will thrive longer than others. In the end, the roots, once the plant is dead, are still roots. They don't disappear; they return to the earth. Their matter may eventually be eaten, or decayed through other means, but they will act as a fertilizer. And that turns into something that was even greater than before.

It's all a cycle. We don't ever truly die. We just change our state of being, the state of our matter.

I'm writing this at 22. My matter is my decrepit awful body. But who I am, that isn't matter. The Being inside of me that IS will live on, produce other things, turn over to different realms and be taken into the universe, because I don't believe that the cycles stop at earth.

I am currently rooted. I am producing, good and bad, but I'm still alive and thriving. Maybe my roots will be cut loose soon, or destroyed, and what my matter is currently would cease to exist. But that's okay. Because I know there's so much more out there. Maybe my roots will thrive for years upon years; only time will tell. But the force of the Universe rules this earth, including the roots within. We are all a part of the Earth, we are all a part of the Universe, serving our own purpose.

Walking with Karma

I was walking with Karma down an all familiar road to regain some balance and clarify what's known.

We spoke about cycles, history, and spiritual growth. Yin and Yang, evolution the most.
When She asked what I had lying heavy on my heart,
Why did I come here, why do I urge for a fresh start?

My failings and teachings are my own to bear, and today that life I live is not why I'm here. I understand patience and reaping what you sow, I also comprehend receiving two-fold.

But while these things make sense and I need no reprise or explanation for why everything makes me cry… I want to know where the justice unfolds? Why do power, greed, status and wealth reign while too many stories of suffering are told? How much longer must we wait to finally see Fate deliver the change we desire?

She continued to walk faithfully by my side, silent until the trails end. She responded to me, finally, by saying
 "dear friend…
You know me too well, your longing is pure, your inquiries clearly aren't of your own. The questions, albeit, make sense to me, the answers aren't mine to be shown. It's Fate you must meet, oh you're in for a treat! She'll get your ducks in a row"

Now, if Karma said to meet Fate, that's my last shot. Going to the place all souls dread is an all too ironic solution; walking back home having left Karma alone, I realized I obtain the key to Fate's layer unknown. I don't need to meet Fate, that day will come. Unwillingly for most, willingly for some. Karma gave me the answers to the questions I posed: Justice will come when Karma meets everyone, and introduces them to Fate...

Behold! Only once you meet Fate, in her abode, will you ever see Justice foretold. Everyone must face Karma... but the Justice you seek cannot be exposed until the deal has been sealed for you to meet Fate through Karma as your vehicle.

Meet Karma, face to face. Stop making her chase you...she's tired. Which is why I go to her, walk with her, and understand her.

Justice is impartial. That's why he's waiting for everyone. He's fair that way you see… But he comes when it's Over, once everyone gotten their key to meet Fate. But no one's ready to turn the key. No one wants to face karma. No one wants IT to be over. No one's ready to meet Fate.

Go. Walk with Karma. She'll give you what you need while we all wait to meet Justice. Decide your Fate. Face your Karma. And you'll see Justice before you know it.

Let Your Spirit Shout

Insane circle, I mean cycle
Try to take a bite full of this pain, engrained and
straining every relation to
Date me awake to the plane of existing in staying
attuned to what we have to
Do, do you feel these sensations from the inside out?
Please
Don't shout me out of the sky, causing me to fall
down to the ground

Meet my Spirit here
It's been a while since she's taken over
It's such a relief, a weight off my shoulders
My heart beats calmly and my brain isn't spiraling
Well, not easily
The weight of this wait took so long to travel through
But now that we're here
I want to come find You

Haze Phase

Addicted to the Haze
because the craze is a phase
the one time in life it's almost predictable,
acceptable, and reprimandable for those who engage,
enrage, turn away, and who heavily play the
Game that doesn't end
it's about leveling up in the timliest of times
because we all know it flys
So fly High in the craze for there are only so many days
Start counting those days for the Game remains but the
players will always change

Shades of Love

Are you there? Do you hear me? I need you, I want you
I'm sorry, I didn't meant it
In desperation, needing reassurance, and manipulation

I'm still here, I hear you
Do you really need me? Are you sure you want me? Do
I make you happy? I forgive you, I adore you, I accept
you for all that you are
With validation, compassion, and respect

Thank you! You've made me excited! I appreciate you!
I'm relieved you know me so well. You're very
thoughtful. I care for you, significantly.

I'd be lost without you. You're everything to me. Don't
leave me.

Wireless Internet

You want internet?

The brain is a computer.

Pre-programmed.

Crack the code.

Disconnect the motherboard.

Rewrite the code.

Restart the program.

Now, you've got 'brainless' connection

Deep Cuts

A razor for the itch
To really get that scratch that's been gnawing at
my ankle for 3 days
A razor for the itch to burn through the blazing
rage and pain I'd rather display on a canvas
What better than my own?
A razor for the itch to trim the fear and fat away
we both will shed for this wedding
A razor for the itch that tears my soul open when
I finally try that recipe and my mouth waters
alongside my eyelids

To Him Every Man (You vs. THEM)

Long-awaited, dream tainted, the
almost-didn't-make-it loop faded, the "never thought
it'd end like this" jaded; Do you see yourself looking
in the mirror, painted? Naked? Suddenly unrelated…

Thou art not of my Kingdom… yet my crown awaits
at your throne. I have left it there for you, until you
join me. If fate had us mate…then marriage should be
our date. I let them out. I'm ready for you to…are
you ready, too?

Self-employed

Reality is your finest creation

Perception is your finest tool

Perspective is your greatest 1-UP

Happiness is your greatest accomplishment.

Self-Love is your Saving Grace

Unconditional love is your Lifeline

Make your job(s) revolve around your life, not the other way around

Silent Auction

Ohm
Home
Shallom
Tommy TuTone
Moooooooaaaaaaannnnnn
Stone Groan
THROW ME A FUCKING BONE
Home-Alone
Ohm

I can spill poetry out of my mouth like a lawnmower spits
out cut grass...

Yet I can never utter the words to demand my true appeal

What do I want or need? What I decide to do with who?

But I see truth and light when the world performs for me,
so why not perform back?

Do the dance, make the appeal

Seduce the world into submission

You won't need words, anyway.

Pressure

The pressures I put on myself to be a good girlfriend, wife, fiancé to you; to keep your dick wet and your stomach full. The pressures I put on myself for you to come home to a home to come home to, have the sheets clean, and bed made…and the laundry put away too. Because my parents fought, played their roles, one marriage didn't work out, the other… well it continues to unfold.

It's not your fault, none of this said in vain, this is not me sitting here cursing your name…
I'm mad I'm angry I'm glad it's all over but the pressures I still carry over my shoulders, our brain patterns and cycles from long long ago (I wish I could tear a bitch up) but I'm so ready to let go. Trying to let the weight go, I end up letting too much weight go I'm back down to 98/99 pounds because I decided to fuck around and play the games the old patterns used to serve me so fucking well.

I don't wanna always have sex, and I don't always tell you things right away, but I know that I'm allowed my privacy and my shame. You've always accepted both and never invalidated one, but with the other, you've smothered it some.

My vibrancy calls to you and you've played its cord,
so now all of these pressures I put on myself are
making me bored.

www.ingramcontent.com/pod-product-compliance
Lightning Source LLC
LaVergne TN
LVHW010949200726

843509LV00013B/2341